TALES of Agony

MURMURS INTO SOLACE

A BOOK BY

MARUSHA ROUF

BlueRose ONE.com
Stories Matter
NewDelhi • London

BLUEROSE PUBLISHERS
U.K.

For permissions requests or inquiries regarding this publication, please contact:

BLUEROSE PUBLISHERS
www.BlueRoseONE.com
info@bluerosepublishers.com
+4407342408967

ISBN: 978-93-6783-304-9

Cover design: Daksh
Typesetting: Tanya Raj Upadhyay

First Edition: February 2025

DEDICATION

To myself,

For the strength and courage to embrace every moment—past, present, and future

For the resilience to rise after every fall,

For never losing hope, even when the journey felt uncertain.

This collection is a reflection of my growth, my struggles, and my unwavering belief in the beauty of life.

As Allah says in the Qur'an:

فَإِنَّ مَعَ الْعُسْرِ يُسْرًا

(Surah Ash-Sharh, 94:6), translates to "Indeed, with hardship comes ease".

This verse became my anchor, a truth that I clung to in my darkest moments. It reminded me that no matter how overwhelming the trails, ease is always waiting just around the corner. Today, I stand with peace in my heart, grateful for the lessons learned and the strength I have gained.

It is also a tribute to my scars, the silent witnesses of battles fought and lessons learned. They no longer burden me but shine as marks of the confidence I've earned.

And to those who are still carrying their pain, this is for you. To everyone who have suffered, endured, and survived—these poems are dedicated to your strength, your resilience, and your quiet bravery.

May this book bring you an emotional, mental and spiritual healing and remind you that no matter the obstacles, there's always a way forward.

ACKNOWLEDGEMENT

بِسْمِ اللَّهِ الرَّحْمَنِ الرَّحِيمِ.

In the name of Allah, the Most Gracious, the Most Merciful

I would like to begin by expressing my deepest gratitude to Almighty Allah, whose guidance and inspiration have been the foundation of my strength. It is through His subtle hints and grace that I was able to create this collection of poems. Allah has given me the opportunity to not only write but also offer a hand, a shoulder, to those readers who will connect with my work. I hope that through these words, I can touch their hearts, make them feel my emotions, and let them find a piece of themselves in my writing. I am truly grateful to Allah for allowing me to embark on this journey and lay the foundation for my poetry. I also want to thank my parents—especially my father, whose financial support has helped push this project forward, and my mother, whose emotional support has been a constant source of strength. To my brother, sister, and the entire family who have always supported me, I am deeply thankful. I'm also grateful to M^{2}ARBS^2 group of seven beautiful souls with whom I have spent my cherished childhood and who have inspired me in every phase of my life. Their encouragement and belief in me continue to push me to develop my writing and growth. A special shout out to Blue Rose Publication and their team for recognizing my talent and providing me the opportunity to express my thoughts. Their support has been invaluable . Finally, to those who are very special to my heart, whose advice has left an indelible mark on me. The guidance they provided was so profound and beautiful that I follow it and would encourage others to do the same, for it can truly help anyone become a better person.

I would also like to extend my gratitude to the authors who have inspired me to become a writer. Shimaz fatima, whose words resonate with me deeply, has been a guiding force. The works of Rumi, John Keats, Fyodor Dostoevsky, and my favorite poet Emily Dickinson have all shaped my understanding of literature and life. Their artistry has been a source of endless inspiration and learning.

I would also like to thank my greatest teachers of all the time–nature and time. Nature has shown me things that no human could, from its patience to its resilience, and beauty in its rawest from, continuously inspiring my journey. Time has been my most constant guide, teaching me to grow, heal, find peace in the moment of chaos. For all the lessons they have imparted, have shaped my perspective, and for that, I am eternally grateful.

I once believed that no one could truly encourage me or show me the path I needed to take. But when I looked around, I found people who cheered me on, who told me that I could do anything, and that there was nothing in the world I couldn't achieve. These individuals provided me with the resources, the support, and the belief I needed. Today, I write this acknowledgment not only to thank them, but to recognize the cherished moments they helped me create. Their encouragement and unwavering faith in me have shaped this journey, and for that, I am deeply appreciative."

-----THANK YOU

FOREWORD

This collection of poems is more than just verses on paper—it's a reflection of my journey through the complexity of emotions. Writing these poems has been a cathartic process for me, allowing me to express feelings I could never quite communicate out loud. As an introvert, I've always found it difficult to share my thoughts, but poetry became my voice when words failed me.

I began this book with the intention of speaking to teenagers and young adults—those who often find themselves navigating the turbulence of emotions, self-identity, and relationships. But as I wrote, I realized that these poems resonate with anyone who has ever experienced the weight of giving their all and receiving nothing in return. For those who have felt the ache of loving without reciprocation, and the internal conflict of wanting to hate the things they love just to escape the grip of attachment.

Through these poems, I have also shed light on deeper emotions—my tears, frustrations, and prayers for the world. Decades of pain for tragedies like Palestine are etched into these words, as are the spiritual moments that brought me closer to my faith. This book reflects how I began to rediscover myself and align my life with the right path.

This journey has been transformative, not just as a writer but as a person. Day by day, I worked on refining my craft, improving with every verse I wrote. The effort I've poured into this collection is immense, and I hope it speaks to you as much as it healed me.

These poems aren't just mine; they are yours too. They are a conversation between you and me, a way to express the emotions that words alone can't capture. Whether you're a teenager, a young adult, or someone reflecting on your own experiences, you'll find something to connect with in these pages. I invite you to embrace them, let them comfort you, and remember that no matter where you are in life, you are never alone in your struggles.

PREFACE

Every heart has its shadows and storms, its whispers and wounds, its yearning for solace. Tales of Agony, Murmurs into Solace is a journey—a tapestry of emotions woven with threads of pain, hope, and transformation. These poems are not merely words; they are echoes of moments where the soul trembled yet persevered.

Each verse reflects the ebb and flow of life—the agony of loss, the beauty of resilience, and the quiet promise of renewal. Inspired by nature, seasons, and the human spirit, these poems are for those who find beauty in the bitter sweetness of existence.

Some poems in this collection are accompanied by handmade illustrations—visual representations that mirror the soul of the verses. I chose to illustrate only a few because certain emotions demanded a form beyond words. These select visuals breathe life into the words, creating an interplay between art and poetry. Each image is a reflection of the feelings behind the lines, adding depth to the stories I wished to tell.

The stories I tell through these verses begin in despair, where the heart aches and the world feels cold. But even in the darkest nights, there are stars. Each tale carries the gentle murmur of solace—a reminder that even amidst agony, there lies a spark of light waiting to guide us home.

I invite you to immerse yourself in these tales, to let them resonate with your own experiences, and to find within them a sense of connection, understanding, and perhaps, healing. This book is my soul poured onto paper, and I hope it speaks to yours.

TABLE OF CONTENTS

INSIDE OF MY HEART

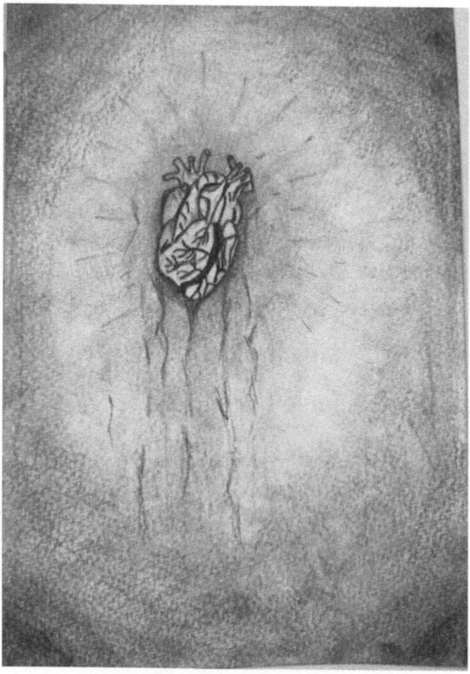

Something is really killing me inside.

I don't know what I have to decide.

I can't express my feelings to anybody.

I'm feeling so depressed.

My heart is in pain; it's really tough to explain.

It drives me all the time insane, and I come and make a complaint,

Why is it with me again?

I want to say something, but my tongue is shivering.

I feel like I'm stuck in chains.

I want to break free and run away.

I want to fight, but I'm feeling so restless.

I want to fly, but I'm feeling so hopeless.

My soul is hungry, which sometimes makes me angry.

I'm not enough strong

I forget where my soul belongs.

Oh God, please help me because I'm drowning.

Please help me because I'm falling.

Please help me because I want to rise.

Please help me because I want to live my life.

I don't want to be bothered by anyone.

I don't want to expect anything from anyone other than you.

I hope that all my wishes will come true.

You will shower the rain of blessings on me, and again I will be happy.

I know that you loved me.

WITHERED

When will my nerves gonna explode?
My brain will stop working.
When will my heart stop beating?
My legs will not walk anymore.

When will my face become numb?
My tongue would feel drought.
When will I lose my emotions?
My tears will stop.

When will I not talk that much?
My speech will be gone.
When will I lie on the bed like a log?
For me, it would be a crown.

When will my sadness go away?
for how much time I have to suffer?
I only have to survive
with numbness, numbness, and numbness.

LOST GIRL

Out of the window, every day, a girl sees the blue sky surrounding her eyes.

The garden is full of desires, and she waits for the sunrise, forgetting about all the lies.

Light fills the corner, and she loves to stay there,

But they dragged her into a raven, which was crowded, yet no one was there.

She heard the noises and knocked the wall a hundred times, but they just made excuses.

"Wait, not right now, maybe sometime later," the words were thrown on her face.

Her emotions rolled down in the form of tears,

But no one sees, and no one cares.

And why should they?

Care for someone like her? The world is hoping for the best for someone else.

The provider doesn't want to see her in pain.

All she wanted was to feel safe, but her soul was burning in hell.

She didn’t know how, where, or when.

She said, "I lost myself in these few days.

I lost someone very strangely.

My hopes, my tears, my trust, my dignity

were craving for a hand that could give me support."

Whenever she sees the road desolated,

She thinks that it is good to be isolated.

The story of her life is very short.

She wanted to see the world full of happiness,

But she was neglected every time.

She stepped into her garden and cried for many hours,

Step by step, she was hoping for good as she plucked some flowers

for herself, to make a crown.

Her beautiful eyes, her Cheshire smile were perfect.

Everyone told her, "What is her problem?"

But no one gives her a solution.

She lost her battle in that pollution,

Coating the walls with whitewash

To hide those mistakes that were printed back in time.
She did her best and kept saying that it will be fine.

Maybe someday she would get some appreciation.
She was tired and hoping for the best.
She wanted to escape and leave her past on the rest.
The days were getting longer and longer,
By the time, she made herself look stronger.

And she said, "Maybe one day, these struggles will be perished,
So I could hold the knob of the door
That will take me to my dreams.
The feeling of depression will flow with the stream.
I will spread my wings in the sky.
I will run with the winds.
I will pour like rain.
I will be a thunder with lightning.
And the whole world will capture the beauty of sparkling."

WHY DOES IT FEEL LIKE

Why does it feel like
My past has drawn me to my past?
Why does it feel like
I'm carrying the baggage of my lies?
Why does it feel like
I can't borrow a piece of happiness from my Lord?
Why does it feel like
This world has turned me down?
Why does it feel like
I'm foisted on this universe?
Why does it feel like
My past is my sniper?
Why does it feel like
My pleasure is gone?
Why does it feel like
My peace is torn?

Apart from this world
Why does it feel like
My selflessness has killed me,
Thrilled me from my past?

Why does it feel like
My heart sheds tears instead of love?
Why does it feel like
My eyes shed poison instead of tears?
Why does it feel like
My hands shed blood instead of support?
Why does it feel like
My limbs are not mine anymore?

Why does it feel like
My past has drawn me to my past?
Why does it feel like
My bullet missed the target,
My car ran off track?
Somewhere, I lost the magic.
What I had was a time-lapse.

Why does it feel like
I don't own my body,
No control over my soul?
Wandering all this time,
Lost from when—I don't know.

I try to find my way, although

I get further intertwined,

Despair deeper in my mind.

Do I have ages—or just tomorrow?

This poem blooms with the creativity of two souls

By Me and SF

BEFORE THIRTEEN

We used to play in the ground nearby your house.
Maybe you have forgotten about it,
But my heart remembers completely.
Some weird games,
Like ice water to play.
So many other habits that I don't like of yours,
But I didn't express it because you were my friend.
Maybe u didn't see how much I neglected all your mistakes throughout our friendship,
But this ship was sailed in dead sea.
That you were so blind and you couldn't see,
You couldn't feel.
I don't know why,
Why were you supposed to tell lies?
I gave myself some time to heal,
But till now, your blind box is sealed.
I ignore, ignore and ignore,
But before thirteen ....

TEENAGER ME

Telling the teenager me,

Why are you worried about the things that never existed?

Don't care; because it's all in vain.

Nothing remains the same; everything has changed.

Telling the teenager me,

Conscience is dead, ethics are gone.

Nothing stays forever.

No one stayed by your side; you were left alone.

All you gained in the cold world was like a cursed bond.

Telling the teenager me,

imagination is good, but face reality

if you want to be safe from the world's cruelty.

Telling the teenager me,

Don't waste your precious things on anyone

Who doesn't deserve it, so let's just preserve it

Telling the teenager me,

Enchanted is just a word with a wonderful feeling,

But no one understands the real thing hidden inside its meaning.

Telling the teenager me,

You've made yourself look like a cager,

putting others first for years.

Now they feel like strangers.

Telling the teenager me,

It hurts deeply inside the heart.

Remember, I told you before,

But you were the only one who chose to start.

Telling the teenager me,

You are the one who built it so high, but you are the only one who brought it down from the sky.

You'll be loved only if you're useful,

or they will judge you by your visuals

Telling the teenager me,

Don't make anyone your inspiration;

They can't see your dedication.

Behind your smiley face,

They don't know what you're hiding

Or with how many lies you're fighting.

Telling the teenager me,
Without your presence, I was stable,
But now it's the opposite.

Telling the teenager me,
Love yourself, have some values,
forget about everything.
So please shall you?

Telling the teenager me,
Being mature isn't rude.
Don't give up; everything will be good.
Life is about earning some food,
So enjoy life and be cool dude

Telling the teenager me,
Sometimes you act creep, but that's okay you don't have to get rid of it
Your presence makes me happier,
Even if you've done things you shouldn't.

Telling the teenager me,
I have a question: Can you answer me honestly?
Sometimes it feels like you're craving for something,

But your tongue is locked; I know there's so much to talk about.

Telling the teenager me,
Shut the door, open your eyes in the dark,
You'll give me many testimonies to be remarked.

Telling the teenager me,
It's okay to feel lonely at night,
To not follow anyone's path,
To be a little one with a subtle smile,
To feel immature because situations are not like that anymore

Telling the teenager me,
Be yourself, rather than faking
Be alert for your future; you don't know what they are plotting
Breaking promises makes you feel like a traitor that I used to hate.

Telling the teenager me,
Pray for yourself from the world's creator,
as there will be no one by your side as your caretaker.

Telling the teenager me,
I want to see you as a shining star,

So my heart can heal from every scar.
Reach a level where you can differentiate
between the hell and the heaven.
Fight for your rights; this is the crucial phase of the life.

Telling the teenager me,
Awake from your deep sleep,
Hide your secrets, stop living in the grief,
Because as they sow, so shall they reap.

ILLUSION

Remembering that day when my heart was crumbled,
My tears were lingering, and my body was rumbled.
They gave me sympathy, that was totally empty,
Never showed me the correct way and said, “it’s okay.”

They said, “it’s the right time,”
And I got trapped into their fatal smiles.

They said, "What's the matter?" and then all my secrets scattered.

I was telling myself that I am fine, but in my mind, I was lying.

That's why the famous author said that love is blind.

I set out on a journey to find my own destiny,

To make it high like a tall tree, and it feels like a fantasy.

BETTER TO BE ALONE

Rather than grabbing your hands and holding on tight,
It's better to be alone.
Rather than crying in your embrace
And leaning my head against you,
So I keep telling myself it's better to be alone.
Rather than relying on your shoulder,
I'll be resting on my hope.
So I keep telling myself it's better to be alone.
Instead of being with you,
I would rather uphold my cane;
I won't keep fake promises and drive you insane.
So I keep telling myself it's better to be alone.

As the sea needs a shore, so as I need you;
As a tree needs its roots, so as I need you;
As the sky needs its pillar, so as I need you;
As barren land needs water, so as I need you;
As birds need their nests, so as I need you;
As a heart needs its beat, so as I need you.
That's why I keep telling myself it's better to be alone.

WHITE SHROUD

Wish I could wrap myself around
In solitude, but out of the town.
Shut the voices up, by taking some sleep at the bottom of the ground
The whisper of silence rings in my ear,
far away from agony, no led out of fear.
White shroud encloses me up, fading of damsel and distress,
Time spends with rest.
With me, fall doze off.
Echoes of turmoil vanishes in the depth,
Deeper in my mind,
laughing out of joy.
Creatures down in the soil are eating my flesh.
Soul wandering in the sky,
roaming around the heavens.
Swing on the moon,
Gazing at the stars,
Dancing in the night,
and sneaking in the clash.
Far away from riots,
Sprinkle some water when chaos ignites.

Sprinting horse with a splendid view,
the souls revolving in the spiritual realm.
Back and forth wealth should not be chased,
The tales of serendipity remain unfazed.

GLIMPSE OF HIDE AND SEEK

I don't know where you are hiding,
Behind the bushes or under the tree,
above the soil or beneath the sea.
You put the keys aside and want to be homebody
At the back of a door or on an open window,
Watching the serene sky or finding tranquillity.
You have been forged in fire, frozen in ice,
You are light for fireflies,
which gathers around you.
You are like oxygen to a bonfire,
keeping it warm.
You are a candle that shows the light of the straight path,
A guide for our belief,
A speciality that no one can see.
Follow the path to the creator;
Read the poem, as if I am your narrator.

In the shadowed cities of the world,
You are the glimmer of hope.
In a world of loud noises,
You stand out as a symbol of grace.
In a world of unwanted meddles,

You never intrude upon someone's space.
In a world full of deceit that runs rampant,
You stand as the emblem of integrity.
In a world of countless deities,
You devote your life to the essence of singularity.
In a world rife with trivial chatter,
You share your wisdom in a profound way.
In a tempest of rage,
You stand out as unfurling petals of patience.

Everyone's so green with envy,
Dreaming of being like me, but alas, their aspirations will forever remain out of reach.
You are the cast of luminous truth in this world;
All seek to mirror your every quality

HIDDEN VOICES

Lost in my dreams while remembering you,
All of a sudden, I saw a glimpse of sunshine through my window.
My garden, which was always gloomy,
You spread some water and made it bright and blooming.

So I open my eyes and hear that angelic voice,
which brings me happiness of zillion times.
Sometimes I'm mad and rude,
But when I see you, you set up my mood.

I know behind your laugh and giggles,
There's so much pain because your loved ones are far away.
As a leader, you're doing well,
There are so many things I want to say.

Your leadership quality is great and wise,
As you bring rise to many smiles.
I want to stay with you as a STAY,
And just stay with me for this whole day.

BOUND TO YOU

Hadn't I never been bound to you,
I wouldn't have ever soaked my soul into depth of sorrow.

Hadn't I never been bound to you,
I wouldn't have ever connected with you like a cosmic web.

Hadn't I never been bound to you,
I wouldn't have ever taken a wound from you.

Hadn't I never been bound to you,
I wouldn't have ever wished for you.

Hadn't I never been bound to you,
I wouldn't have ever visited your place

Hadn't I never been bound to you,
I wouldn't have ever met you as time passed by.

Hadn't I never been bound to you,
I wouldn't have ever called you my soul mate.

Hadn't I never been bound to you,
I wouldn't have ever prioritized you.

Hadn't I never been bound to you,
I wouldn't have ever knocked at the door.

Hadn't I never been bound to you,
I wouldn't have ever asked for your support.

Hadn't I never been bound to you,
I wouldn't have ever pleaded for you to stay.

Hadn't I never been bound to you,
I wouldn't have ever let a wave decay.

Hadn't I never been bound to you,
I wouldn't have ever let you go away.

NUMBNESS

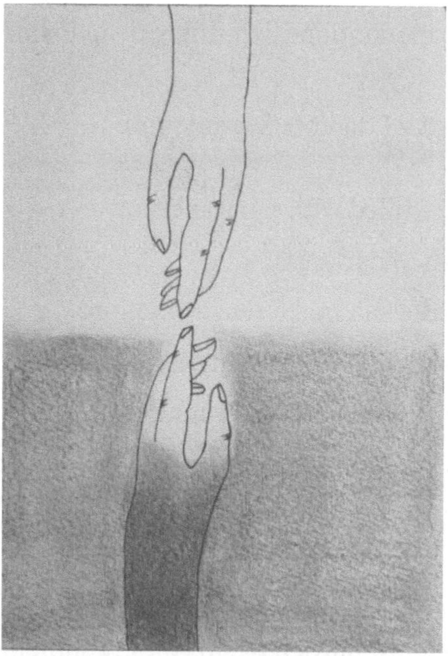

Something suspicious is going around,

but I can't reach it.

My body is shaking, and my heart is cuffed.

I'm still a child, not knowing that life is going to be rough.

I'm feeling that I have lost something very special.

Going too far doesn't make sense anymore.

I'm feeling the lowest of my imaan right now;
I can't take it anymore.
Falling into pieces doesn't seem relatable.
A mixture of emotions is running deep inside my head.
Being loved-- I don't feel it anymore.

Corners are filled with ignorance;
Light is full of darkness.
Gratitude doesn't make sense anymore.
I don't feel my heart feels anything.
Life is going in a merry-go-round direction.
Sorrow is irresistible.

I think I have lost my stability.
It's like you snatched my peace and tranquility.
There is a lot of burden of sins on my shoulders,
But I have misplaced my taqwa.
It's like I have killed my own soul.
Now I feel numb and a spirit without a goal.

Counting numbers and signs that you gave me about my intuition,
You told me “Don't waste your thoughts on anybody.”
But I'm feeling tired; I don't know what to do.
Bring me back to me and erase all scars that I gifted to myself.

Remorse of everything is getting worse day by day.

I can't forget all those mistakes that I have made.

Lonely hands are smiling in pain;

Tears in my eyes are worthless these days.

Memories are fading away in my mind, but my heart captured

Those lies swirling in my soul, and my hopes are ruptured.

Blocked vision couldn't see anything.

Behind your back, there was so much joy waiting for me.

Got stuck in your illusion.

Don't know what to write or think;

Right now, I'm completely sunk

In my thoughts, I always saw you as my creative vision.

The bond that I shared with You is on the verge of vanishing.

Feeling sorry for myself,

helplessness has mounted on my thoughts.

I hope that all my memories will get perished.

I don't know why it's always one-sided friendships

That quickly comes to an end ship.

Scattered in my own eyes,

Guilty grief running down due to a fear

That I couldn't treat You better,

Didn't give you what You deserve.

You are like a treasure that I'm going to lose;

Without your talks, I don't know what I have to choose.

Without Your advice and care, I would feel completely alone.

This is a goodbye to all my memories that I shared with you.

May God bless You in every field of hardship.

Life is way too long, and someone is waiting for You there.

You tried your best to change me,

Gave me a better version of myself.

These years, you and I may have gone through a lot,

But you told me change is a part of life.

Maybe it would take some time to get accommodated with people.

You told me not to leave your salah;

You taught me how to remain on your taqwa.

It will take time to forget what you mean to me.

In the early days, I discovered the presence of Your kindred soul.

Soon, I found my inspiration in You, and a rare friendship took hold.

As time passed, You taught me how to deepen my connection to the divine.

After some time, You taught me that emotional ties also remain confined.

Eventually, I learned that every bond may drift away,

but memories often stay.

The people may come and go, but lesson imprints remain.

Stay as who I am, laughing through joy and pain.

Glossary

Imaan : trust on Allah/ god

Taqwa: Piety, God - consciousness

Salah: prayer, an Islamic practice to worship

MY BELOVED

When I was torn apart,
He gave me hope at last,
But I neglected His mercy
And thought it was naturally.

There was loath around,
And I was collecting my pieces from the ground.
He gave me light in the dark,
But I neglected His mercy
And thought it was naturally.

When I was unsatisfied,
He gave me satisfaction all the time,
But I neglected His mercy
And thought it was naturally.

When I was perplexed,
He told me to relax.
Every time, I neglected His mercy
And thought it was naturally.

But one day, suddenly,
A voice came and asked me,

"Why can't you destroy the barriers between you and Me?
Why can't you grab My rope and hold on?"

I was in shock.
Then I saw it was ten o'clock.
I took my pillow,
Put it under my head and said,
"I want to go to bed."

Every time, I neglected His mercy
And thought it was naturally.

Then I cried so much out of pain,
Thinking my heart was full of stains.
Then He said,
"Call upon Me, and I will respond to you.
Take one step towards Me, and I will take ten towards you.
If you need Me, I'm always there for you.
If you want to repent, I will forgive you.
If you forget Me, I will be waiting for you."

At that moment,
I felt like the sun's rays pierced through the clouds.
From that day,
He became my beloved.

WHAT LIFE IS ALL ABOUT

It's all about suffering and it's all about pain,
It's all about being hurt and it's all about to be in vain,
It's all about to stop and it's all about to hate,
It's all about to be judged and it's all about to be rain,
It's all about being sad and it's all about being unhappy,
It's all about being asleep and it's all about to be to try again

HOME

I drifted myself from door to door,
But I always found you at my home.

I looked at the sky and searched for you,
But I always find you at my home.

I always thought I'd meet you at the dome of heaven,
But still, I ended up finding you at my home.

I searched for you in the holy gardens,
But again, i found you at my home.

I explored you in my thoughts,
But I found you at my home.

I hunted you inside my dreams,
But I always found you at my home.

I seek for you in palace of greenery,
But I only found you at my home.

I outlined you in the written stories,
But I only found you at my home.

I drifted myself from door to door,
But yet, I only found you at my home.

HE IS WITH THOSE WHO ARE PATIENT

We were once met by chance,
or maybe by mistake.
I'm waiting for the day,
when we will once again turn into decay.

No matter how far I have to travel,
for you, I will cross the seven seas.
I will grasp your hand and take you down with me,
towards infinity,
where He will maintain our modesty.

He will purify you and me,
concealing our duties.
one step toward positivity,
to live the life of eternity.

So till then, let's be patient for a while.
Let's put the things back aside.
Let's end this story with:
"Inna Allaha Ma' As-Saabireen".
(Al Baqrah:2:153)

I HAVE CRIED FROM PAST FEW DECADES

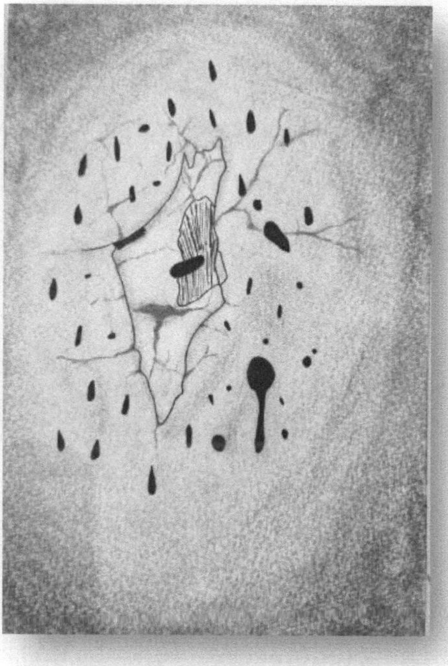

The tears in my eyes, which I can't forget,
And you can't see,
The missiles that you led to my home,
All those countries that saw my pain when I was enduring it all alone

I have cried from past few decades,

The massacre unfolds in a cascade
They took my freedom to live their life,
They took my soul and burned it alive,
They took my precious place.
Today is the situation that I can't even face,

I have cried from past few decades,
I have buried my beloved ones with my own hands,
I have kept crying for so many hours for my own land,
to be free from genocide.

Oh Allah, we are so terrified,
My heart is suffering to see those hands,
Crying inside the rubble,
O Muslim world, you have to assemble."
We say we are great, our beloved Prophet(PBUH)has stepped on this land.
From Al-Aqsa, they have travelled up above seven heavens.
They moved in this space just to make it expand
We are searching for other AL- Khatab(RA) and another Ayubi.
Some are waiting for the arrival of Mehdi.
Scream with the name of Allah turns into people's plea,
As the chants speak across the whole world:
"From the river to the sea,
Palestine will be free."

FLY HIGH

Things have slipped from my grasp now,
And I'm uncertain of when or how.
It all seems so unreasonable to me;
I struggle to see things clearly.

I can overlap my hatred with my love,
And wanted to travel the world with wings like a dove
I seek to understand my feelings,
as the wounds of my heart are healing.

I once believed all miseries had gone.
I fought with desires until the last dawn.
I don't wish to hold grudges;
I want to embrace a happier life.

I want to fly with my wings in the beautiful open sky,
To lift myself truly high
He has written my destiny,
And I trust that it will be clear and satiny

STRONGER

Feel the pain, embrace the night,
The things you possess may not be right.
Find your own shelter, fill your life with glitter,
Do what you want, when they hurt you a lot.

Push them away from your fate;
They can't decide because it's too late.
Stand firm where you belong,
Forget the past; it's gone.

Be stronger than you've ever been,
Be a precious one to yourself, like you've never seen.
Though times are hard, they'll end soon,
Then you'll shine bright, like a radiant moon

IT'S OKAY

If you care about someone, it's okay if they don't care back.
If you give sympathy to someone, it's okay to be rejected.
If you have a quaint type of nature, it's okay to be introverted.
If you don't like to stay in a crowd, it's okay to be isolated.

If you give advice to someone just to show your affection,
It's okay to be neglected.
When you don't laugh at their futile jokes,
They may say you're bizarre, but don't be offended.
Because It's okay to be unique.

When you don't share the secrets you've kept in your heart,
They may say you can trust us, but it's okay to be self-centered.
It's okay to not dress properly.
It's okay to be a mess.

This world wants to set new rules for you,
They want you to follow its cues,
But always do that what suits you.

24 JUNE

This day comes out every year,
But it doesn't make me happy now.
I have to do a lot of work,
But I can't help myself now.

These days make me insecure,
Weak, vulnerable, and show me that I'm still astray.
There are so many wishes for me,
But only for one day, and I know I have to make it pay.

I need something that gives me peace for a second at least.
That thing will be so precious to me, more than anything.
It will be a ray of light for me,
And it will give me a good sight to see.

All I want is you to pray for me,
So I can spend the rest of my life happily.

14TH MAY

You are my Sunrise, you are my sunshine.

You are the peace of my heart, you are the beautiful sign of my life.

When I see you everyday, you make my day bright.

Your alluring smile with those pleasing eyes

Give me another reason to rise to become greater and wise.

In your arms, I always feel my home.

I wish I could make them my own.

I wish I could live with you forever.

You always came as a ray to redeem me and make a nice weather.

I wish I could give you a promise of an eternal life.

So that only death can put us apart.

As he said, "Heaven lies beneath your feet."

You always show mercy and never get a defeat.

Oh, my beloved mother, I always want to be yours and you to be mine.

But it saddens me a little bit when you are not fine.

You always suppressed your feelings for us,
so that you could gain our love and trust.
I want to tell you, that all sacrifices you made when you were suffering from pain,
I will not let it go in the vain and I will make your scars go away.

When I see you smiling, my all sorrows disappear.
When I hold your hand, I don't feel scared.
But I just want you to know that I will become a bridge to catch your dreams,
So that all of your stress would be healed,
And you will sigh with big relief.

M^2ARBS^2

I had no dreams; they taught me how to stay brim.

I was lost in the dark; they taught me how to smile.

My heart was broken and sad; they gave me the sympathy I never had.

When it seemed so blurred to me, they made it clear.

When problems struck me to the end, they always stood by my side.

They taught me how to fight.

They taught me how to become a light.

They taught me to stay strong when my fears tore me apart.

They grabbed my hand and held it when I was losing myself.

They gave me hope on how to rise.

They are air- spread souls, where I find my scared solace.

HATE YOU

Wish I could hate you, but you live under vast serene sky.

Wish I could hate you, but the uproar of river flows nearby.

Wish I could hate you, but my ears capture you melodious wave.

Wish I could hate you, but the way your artistry has paved the way.

Wish I could hate you, but you alchemize dark shadows into light's embrace.

Wish I could hate you, but caressing of yours turns horde into empty space.

Wish I could hate you, but you give the sense of equilibrium.

Wish I could hate you, but you keep your wavelengths in the hollow spectrum.

Wish I could hate you, but your intertwined speech gives life a fractal design.

Wish I could hate you, but your veiled trove is the tender mercy.

Wish I could hate you, but your aura brings a celestial bright.

Wish I could hate you, but the lantern flickers the virtuous sight.

Wish I could hate you, but your noble spirit weaves into harmony.

Wish I could hate you, but you endlessly sow the seeds of wisdom,

giving rise to beautiful cohesive symphony.

THE UNEXPRESSED ONE

With many laughs and giggles, let's end it with a goodbye.
With many mesmerizing memories, let's end it with a goodbye.
From creating conflicts to summarising them, let's end it with a goodbye.
From correcting my grammar to changing the topic,
"By ignoring some words, you make it ironic."
"From listening to my struggles to offering solutions," let's end it with a goodbye.
As I was a dominant, to an apologetic one,
From being a motivator to reassuring me,
From being insensitive to becoming unexpressed,
As I was an angry bird to an emotional one,
Let's end it with a goodbye.
I was the darkest shade, so you were my reflective one.
I was intensive, so you were my frozen one.
As I was chaotic, you were my ordered one.
As I was into nothingness, you were my complete one.
As I was the black hole, you were my event horizon.
In this dim air, you are my brightest star.
In the constellations, you are the picture of calmness.
In the crowd of war, you are an act of silence.

In the world of liars, you are an act of honesty.
In this harsh reality, you are an act of sobriety.
This is only an assumption for you,
which is obviously not so true.
I'm closing this hidden treasure in the soil.
I don't want to admit everything and make it a spoil.
So let's just end everything with a good bye.

AM I THE ONLY ONE TO SAY

Am I the only one to say,
That we are now sitting so far away?
It saddens me that our lives will never be the same again.
Am I the only one to say,
Connected by bridge to bridge, yet still out of reach,
Under the same sky, holding up memories,
in the heart's treasure, dearest to me.
Am I the only one to say,
We cannot wage a war against destiny,
because we are bound by our fates.

Am I the only one to say,
You break my silence of sorrow;
Never shatter my resilience.

Am I the only one to say,
Orchards of joy bring no tomorrow.
I enjoy your delightful presence; wrap me up and give me protection.
Your promises were never fake and hollow.

Am I the only one to say
As you complete my beloved family,

You are the seven stars of this soulful galaxy.

I just want to capture a glance to embellish our eternal gallery.

Am I the only one to say,

My gratitude is never enough;

Don't know how much I am blessed.

I will wait till you return home,

Under the mighty Chinar tree,

Where in nature, we will sit & remain carefree.

A LETTER

Sitting in my room, silently staring at a clock,
Thinking about you, and suddenly all my thoughts were blocked.
I was making an effort to build our deep bond,
But I was far away from it, and you were already gone.

I adore you so much, I thought that I can't live without you.
As I was a building, you were my plinth.
As I was a moth, you were my light.
As I was a fire, you were the water.
As I was lost, you showed me what was right.
And we shared this common trait.

Whenever I was sad, you brought me joy.
Whenever I was feeling anxious, you brought calm.
Whenever I saw you, my heart felt unique excitement.
And whenever I embraced you, I felt safe in your arms.

All I want is for you to stay in my memories and my life too.
Your motivation makes my heart smile every day.

And from your dedication, you turned every day into a victory.

Remember, I haven't changed; there are some work in which I'm engaged.

I just want to share with you my gratitude.

Thank you for everything you did.

For that, I offer you a heartfelt salute.

Everything you did, I can't repay,

And that's all I want to say.

OH, THE BELIEVER OF ALLAH

Oh, the believer of Allah,
He knows the secret you hide in your heart,
the pain that you endure with a big smile.
From where have you borrowed this art?
The time calls you versatile.
You got a gift which can change people's destiny.
You gather them in a crowd and pour the message of modesty.

You are the inspiration for the youth,
to show them how to follow the cues.
You inspire them with your generosity,
They want to learn with more curiosity.
You are very kind and humble,
You grab them with your words when they are about to stumble.

You got the courage and fear of oneness,
while the world is living in glumness.
Since you have sacrificed your desire and submitted your will to Him,
You are counted amongst the righteous.

Tears buried in your eyes are visible to Him;

He can see the emptiness inside you.
Sometimes it's hard to balance,
every emotion that runs inside your body.
You give away charity,
never getting bound in melancholy by His boundless mercy.

As He says, “They would be measured among infidels.”
He instills fear among you, due to their wicked antics.
He segregates you from them,
Who trade their spirits for hollow ambition,
spreading hateful tactics.

With their false agony,
They weave their stories and lead people astray.
They can't see the truth in front of them,
as they have been blocked by their vision.
But yet, in the realm of darkness, you are honoured as a quasar.

If you will follow the path He has shown,
Surely Elysium and Tartarus will be clearly known.
That place of tranquility will be yours, so pure and bright.
Guided by faith, you will walk in His light.

MAYBE SOME OTHER DAY

Maybe, some other time, I will stay with you—
But not forever, and it will never be the same again.
Maybe, someday, I will be by your side,
But not forever, and it will never be the same again.

Maybe, someday, I will crash into your dreams,
But not forever, and it will never be the same again.

Maybe, someday, I will find somebody,
But not forever, and it will never be the same again.

Maybe, we will get to know each other,
But not forever, and it will never be the same again.
Maybe, someday, I will leave you,
And you will be all alone—
But not forever, and it will never be the same again.

SONG OF VICTORY

Like slow nights that give coverage to the scars,
Like moon swings on the blackness of twilight,
Like stars, which reflect their life on earth,
Like streams flowing in one direction,
Like the willow, because it bends down instead of going up,
Like the Chinar leaves, because they give life to the dead forests,
Like high rides, because it plugs the trigger in,
Like gravity, because it gives the reason to stand still,
Like speed, as adrenaline rush so far,
Like horses, adding loyalty up to the core,
Like secrets, hidden in the safest place.

Bury feelings behind the gaze;
The act of indolence may mask up the ache.
Weep in quietude; seclude those whose words are nothing but waste.
Escapism isn't a way to live; it just makes you numb.
Thus, cease to tend the serpent beneath the sleeves,
For their fun, they render you dumb.
For every misstep, they condemn you for your naivety.
Wield the pointed blade; sword them with creativity.

This system parts the treasure; sincerity is sold.
They gamble with vice, just like silver and gold.

Freedom will come with captivity.
Today's oppressor will be oppressed tomorrow,
When the whole world would hum
And celebrate the song of victory.

DREAMSCAPE ADVENTURE

Wind unleashed, making the trees dance in the cold breeze.

The sky appears like two oceans meet:

The clearer one shows sunrise, and the other sunset.

The season shows a unique kind of glimpse.

The steeds in the meadows, bolting with speed,

Like a roller coaster vibe, unlock the fear to decrease,

Give the eternal peace.

Glacier surrounds the glamorous scenery,

With the echoes in the mountains and forests beside, glorifies the beauty.

The heavy clouds, appearing like cotton candy,

Zoned out but yet with equanimity.

Dew drops cling on the leafy greens,

Still offers reason to survive.

Leave the noisy world; a new journey awaits to start,

By calling out, revive your ethereal part.

SEASONS

Birds are chirping across the branches.
The sunlight strikes, nearly expand through the window.
The pleasant morning makes it easy;
It graze my eyes, and I shall rise from slumber.
The flowers bloom in the sea-blue sky;
Butterflies twirl in between them,
securing their floral essence.
In every season, they return again,
And it feels like, “Finally, spring has awakened from deep dreams.”

As time passes, the sun grows hotter,
Giving off a vibe of Tartarus,
to test our patience.
The ice cream melts down,
And we run towards the light shades.
Under the umbrella,
The nights become more peaceful,
and it feels like, “Finally, that bewildering summer again.”

Soon, it may rain heavily;

The umbrella again returns with a peaceful smile.

The "shhh" sound of rain creates a musical vibe,

as the season of calamity descends from high.

It knocks at the door and finally says,

"Hi there, it's me, monsoon."

And swaps with a goodbye.

After a time, the leaves may dry,

Falling like lifeless golden sheaths,

covering the ground with crispy cracks.

Windows chatter as the mighty storm crashes,

Creating a hustle that disappears in a flash.

Welcoming us with the shift from amber to cruel, frosty time.

Eventually, blankets cover the ground,

And it says, "I'm snow-laden."

It withers the enchanted forest, sparking beauty in spruce,

As bundles of crystals fall from the sky, giving a sense of profuse

Nature's style of gratitude and grace;

Of course, his bounty can't be traced.

GLORIOUS DAYS

Glorious days return to their hub,
but they left their aroma in my mind
I reminisce about the desires in my psyche;
It gives me a little bit of solace.
My heart adds up the flawless memories,
of writing the skeptical stories,
About my tidy flaws,
Falling into parts just like repulsive thoughts.

Nowadays my mind dangles much more than my heart,
from calling for the celebration to dying for it now.
My life lives in the science of the cosmos;
My soul is adrift in sight of the empyrean.
It descends onto my canvas painted with divine energy.
Mystery plays the radical task in everyone's zest;
It is a heavier mess,
And aback it seems much more than less.

The vortex is spacing out in my ancient times.
They say history repeats itself,

Just like it has a comeback and detoured the path again.
Cluster of stains are immersed in the sea of my chest;
It hits the shore, and feels like the cardiac arrest.

Glorious days will return to its path again,
When the tides will collapse within,
When slogans of passion will be raised everywhere,
When flares of flame will be flown in the air,
When the phoenix will ascend from ashes
To renew it into something rare
When the hearts will abide,
when the tempest's rage is blown aside.

In the Glorious days, I reclaim my way,
When our seclusion will be maintained.
In the middle of the voyage, I will unearth my sway.